GREAT MINECRAFT® BUILDS

# YOUR UNOFFICIAL GUIDE TO BUILDING COOL MINECRAFT® RAILROADS

S. D. MORISON

Enslow PUBLISHING

**Please visit our website, www.enslow.com. For a free color catalog of all our high-quality books, call toll free 1-800-398-2504 or fax 1-877-980-4454.**

**Library of Congress Cataloging-in-Publication Data**
Names: Morison, S. D., author.
Title: Your unofficial guide to building cool Minecraft® railroads / S. D. Morison.
Description: New York, N.Y. : Enslow Publishing, [2023] | Series: Great Minecraft builds | Includes bibliographical references and index.
Identifiers: LCCN 2022005437 (print) | LCCN 2022005438 (ebook) | ISBN 9781978529366 (library binding) | ISBN 9781978529342 (paperback) | ISBN 9781978529359 (set) | ISBN 9781978529373 (ebook)
Subjects: LCSH: Minecraft (Game)–Juvenile literature. | Railroads–Juvenile literature.
Classification: LCC GV1469.35.M535 M6728 2023 (print) | LCC GV1469.35.M535 (ebook) | DDC 794.8/5–dc23/eng/20220215
LC record available at https://lccn.loc.gov/2022005437
LC ebook record available at https://lccn.loc.gov/2022005438

Published in 2023 by
**Enslow Publishing**
29 E. 21st Street
New York, NY 10010



Portions of this work were originally authored by Ryan Nagelhout and published as *The Unofficial Guide to Building Railroads in Minecraft*. All new material this edition authored by S. D. Morison.

Designer: Rachel Rising
Editor: Jill Keppeler
Illustrator: Matías Lapegüe

Photo credits: Cover, pp. 1, 3, 4, 6, 8, 10, 12, 14, 16, 18, 20, 22-24 Orange Sky ART/Shutterstock.com; Cover, pp. 1-24 Phoenix 1319/Shutterstock.com; Cover, pp. 1, 3, 8, 10, 12, 14, 16, 18, 22-24 Soloma/Shutterstock.com; p. 4 vlastas/Shutterstock.com; p. 6 KickaPoo/Shutterstock.com; pp. 8, 10, 12, 14, 16, 18 Phoenix 1319/Shutterstock.com; p. 13 dimcha/Shutterstock.com; p. 17 Denis Belitsky/Shutterstock.com; p. 19 f11photo/Shutterstock.com.



Printed in the United States of America



CPSIA compliance information: Batch #CSENS23: For further information contact Enslow Publishing, New York, New York, at 1-800-398-2504.

# CONTENTS

Moving Through Your World . . . . . . . . . . 4
Iron Is Important . . . . . . . . . 6
A Mineshaft Quest . . . . . . . 8
By the Block . . . . . . . . . . . . 10
Means of Moving . . . . . . . . 12
About Redstone . . . . . . . . . 14
More Rails, More Choices . . 16
At the Station . . . . . . . . . . . 18
Imagine This! . . . . . . . . . . . 20
Glossary . . . . . . . . . . . . . . 22
For More Information . . . . . 23
Index . . . . . . . . . . . . . . . . . 24

Words in the glossary appear in **bold** type the first time they are used in the text.

# MOVING THROUGH YOUR WORLD

*Minecraft* worlds are nearly **infinite**. You can travel for thousands of blocks from your **spawn** point in any direction and still not reach the end. This can take many days—both in the game and in the real world! While it can be lots of fun to explore, you might sometimes want to travel **efficiently** from one location to another. This is when railroads can be very handy in *Minecraft*.

The game doesn't have trains, but it does have rails, minecarts, and other items you can use to build a **transportation** system of your own.

Is there a mountain between your base and another site in your *Minecraft* world? Why not build a railway tunnel?

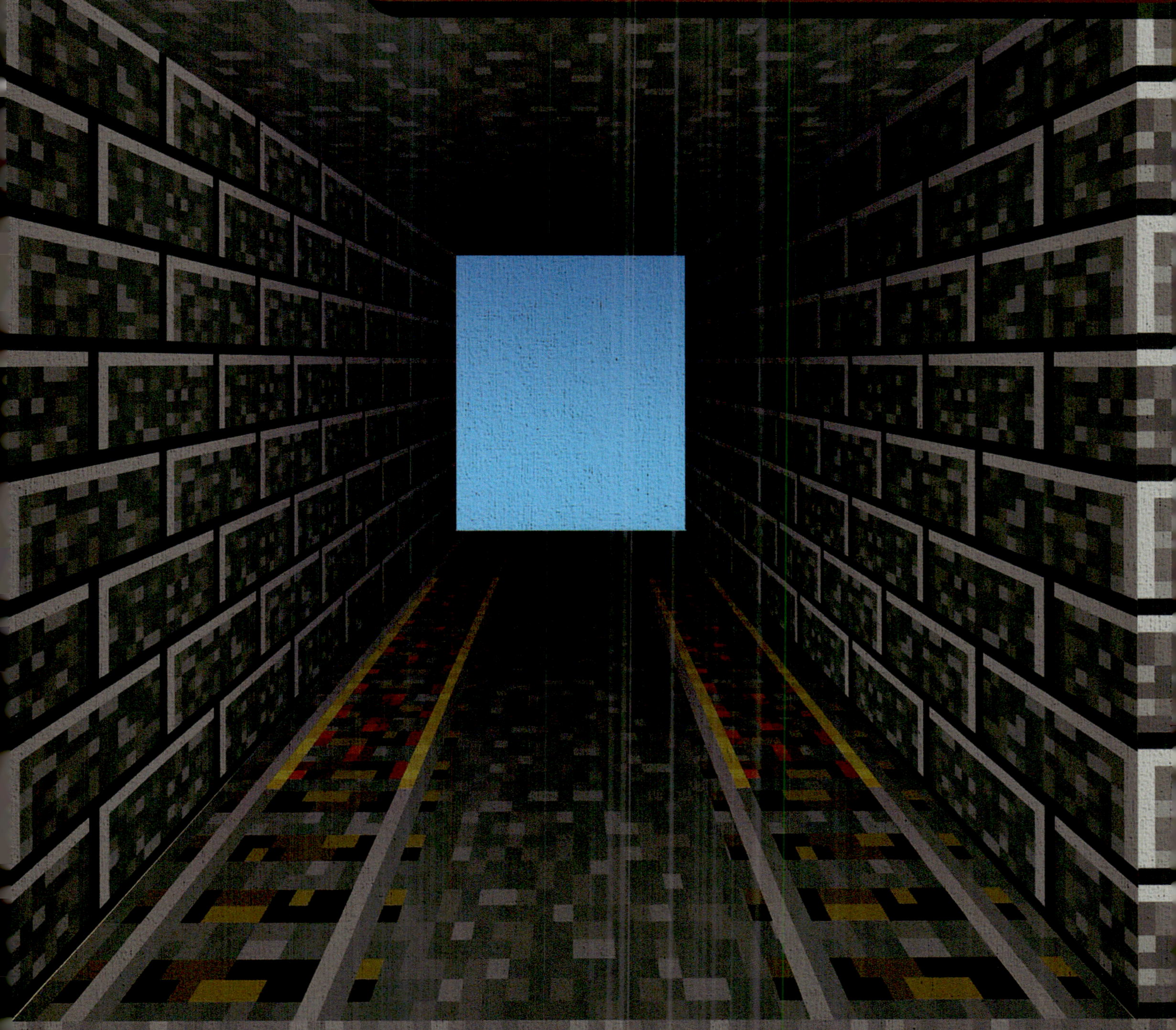

# IRON IS IMPORTANT

While *Minecraft* railways can be very useful, it can take a lot of **materials** to build them. For 16 pieces of plain *Minecraft* rail, you'll need six iron ingots, or bricks, and a stick. And every piece of rail only covers one block! You'll also probably want to make other types of rails that need other materials as well.

To make iron ingots, you need iron ore. These blocks are usually underground and need to be mined. Then you **smelt** the ore in a furnace to make iron ingots.

IRON INGOTS

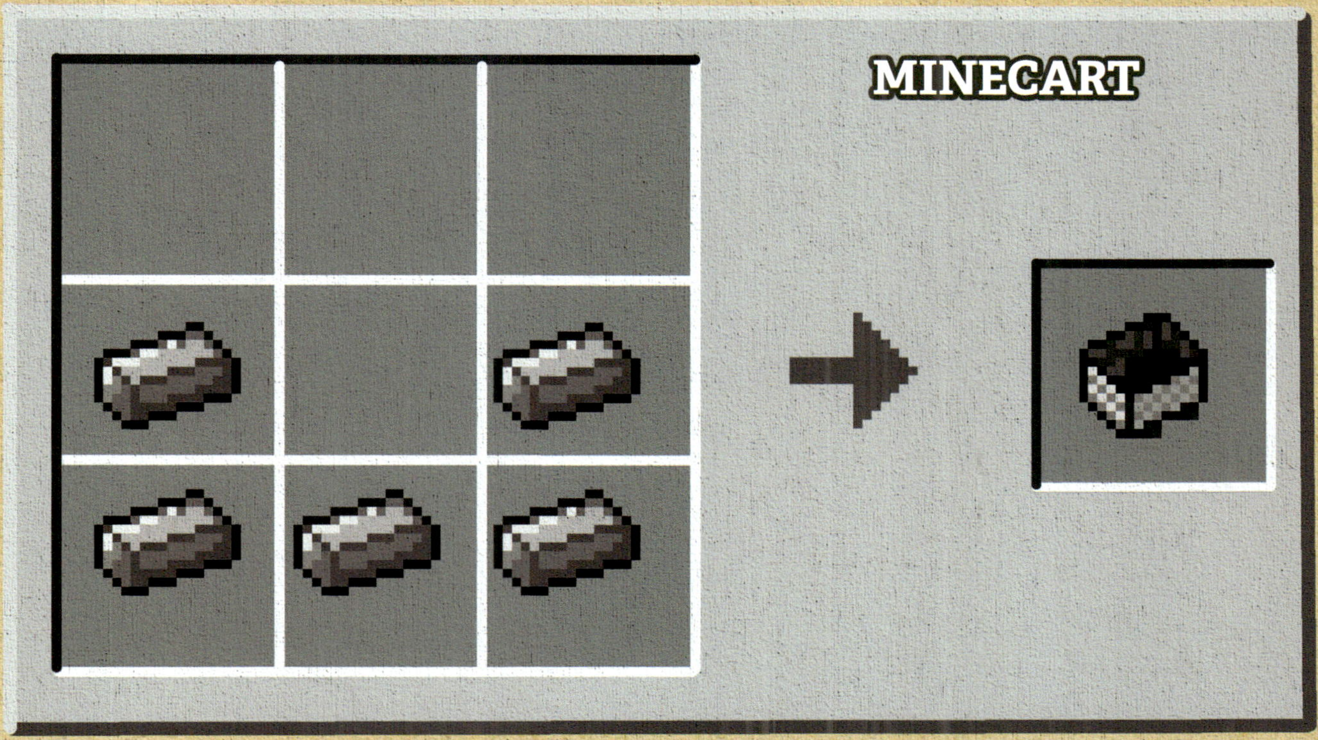


You also need iron to make minecarts to ride in or carry things in. Each minecart needs five iron ingots.

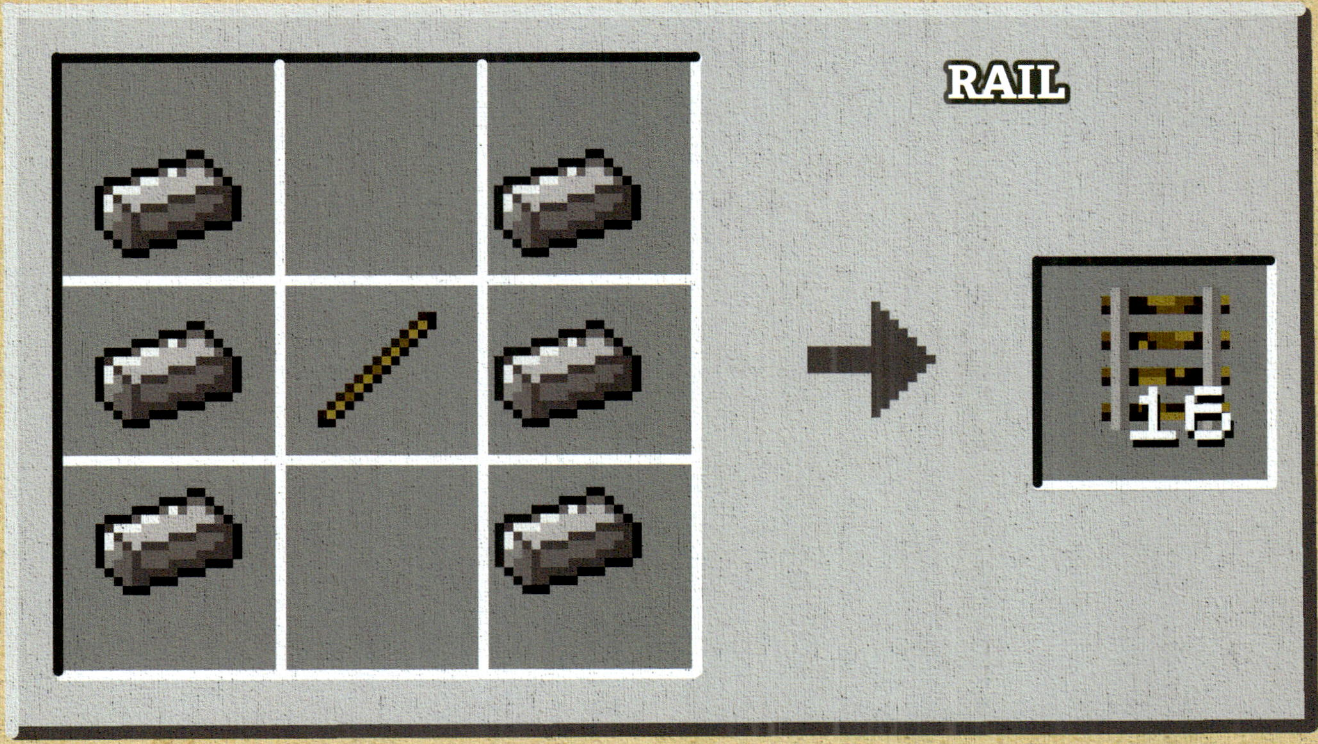

# A MINESHAFT QUEST

It can take a lot of time and effort to gather materials for a *Minecraft* railway of any length. However, there are places in *Minecraft* worlds where rails and minecarts generate, or appear, naturally. You can find these mineshafts underground or sometimes underwater. These mazelike tunnels may also have chests with more minecarts and different sorts of rails.

In badlands **biomes**, which have red sand and terra-cotta blocks, mineshafts can generate right on the surface. All mineshafts also have supports made of planks, or pieces of wood, and fence pieces.

## ADVENTURE MODE

All mineshafts can have cave spiders, a **venomous** type of *Minecraft* spider, and cobwebs. Be careful!

Your *Minecraft* railway builds can be aboveground or underground.

# BY THE BLOCK

*Minecraft* worlds are made up of blocks. There are steady, still blocks such as stone, dirt, and ores. There are also blocks that can flow, like water or lava, or fall, like sand or gravel. You can only place rails on solid (nonliquid) blocks, and only some blocks (including sand or gravel) are affected by **gravity**.

These blocks may not be good surfaces for rails, because if they fall, they can break your rail line. Also, rails will be washed away if water or lava flow over them.

## ADVENTURE MODE

**Basic rails can go straight or turn left or right. They can also go up or down one block at a time.**

LAVA

WATER

SAND

You can build bridges of solid materials such as bricks or stone to go over *Minecraft* **obstacles** such as lava or water.

BRICK

STONE BRICK

# MEANS OF MOVING

Minecarts move along railways. There are a few different types of minecarts in *Minecraft*. Plain minecarts are empty, and players or other mobs can ride in them. You can push another mob into a minecart, or an empty minecart will pick up another mob if it runs into it.

Minecarts can also hold chests to store things, furnaces to power them, hoppers to collect items, spawners to produce mobs, or TNT to blow things up. Remember that different versions, or types, of *Minecraft* may have different features, however.

## ADVENTURE MODE

**In some versions of *Minecraft*, minecarts can hold command blocks. These are special blocks (usually not in survival worlds) that let players use special commands.**

If a moving minecart runs into something on its track, it will reverse its direction, or go the other way.

# ABOUT REDSTONE

You can move a minecart if you're riding in it, to some extent. However, if you want to keep going for a long distance or uphill, you're going to need power. You can make special rails in addition to plain ones. You'll need six gold ingots, a stick, and a piece of redstone dust to make six powered rails.

You can get redstone dust from redstone ore deep underground. (This is also where you'll find most gold ore, which can be smelted to make gold ingots.) Redstone dust can provide power, rather like electricity in *Minecraft*.

## ADVENTURE MODE

Powered rails glow when they're turned on by power sources such as redstone torches (made with one piece of redstone dust and a stick). They can move a minecart up a hill or make it move faster.

When powered rails have a power source, they give a minecart **momentum**. When they don't, they'll slow a moving minecart or bring it to a stop.

# MORE RAILS, MORE CHOICES

There are other sorts of rails in *Minecraft* as well. Detector rails (made from six iron ingots, a stone pressure plate, and redstone dust) give off a power signal when a minecart passes over them. They can also detect, or sense, how full container minecarts are.

Activator rails, when powered by a redstone source, can set off something when a minecart passes over them. For example, if a TNT minecart goes over a powered activator rail, the TNT will blow up! Activator rails are made from six iron ingots, two sticks, and a redstone torch.

## ADVENTURE MODE

**Detector rails can power redstone components, or parts, of various sorts. These components include redstone repeaters, which can carry or control signals.**

With a **lever** (made with a block of cobblestone and a stick), you can switch curving tracks from one direction to another. Keep in mind that only regular rails can curve.

# AT THE STATION

Of course, you'll have a place your railroad starts and a place (or places) where it stops. You'll at least want a block at the end of your rails so your minecarts don't leave the track. You might want a small building (or a large building!) so you have a space for your minecarts or a platform where you can stand to get into minecarts or load them.

Sometimes railroad builds can be very complex, or have many parts. They can go underground, have multiple paths, or set off different actions.

**ADVENTURE MODE**

**If you know you want to build a very complex railroad in *Minecraft*, you might want to play in creative mode. In this mode, you'll have all the materials you could want right at hand.**

Penn (or Pennsylvania) Station in New York City is one of the largest and busiest rail stations in the world. Can you imagine building it in *Minecraft*?

# IMAGINE THIS!

Trains in the real world have engines that pull them and different sorts of train cars. While *Minecraft* minecarts and rails are much simpler, you can still use your imagination to create many different things. For example, you could use blocks to make a train engine for your station, even if it's just for show.

A *Minecraft* railway can be both useful for transportation and for great creative builds. And you can combine the two! Even a simple railway can have some unique, or one-of-a-kind, touches. Have some fun!

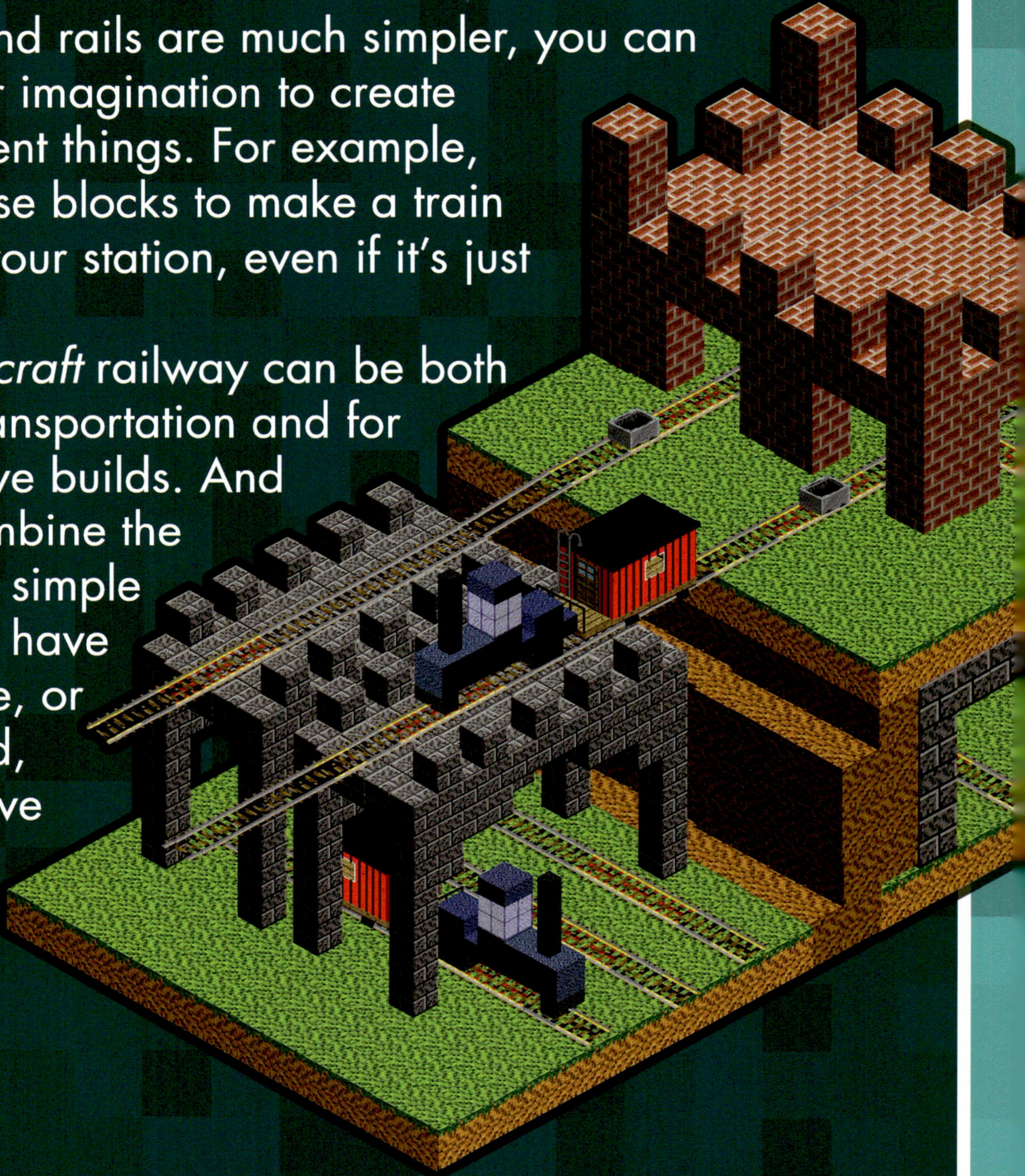

Your *Minecraft* railway can be simple and useful—or it could be a rollercoaster ride!

# GLOSSARY

**biome** A natural community of plants and animals, such as a forest or desert.

**efficiently** Working in a way that's efficient, or capable of producing desired results without wasting results, time, or energy.

**gravity** The force that pulls objects toward the center of a planet or star. The force that pulls objects toward Earth's center.

**infinite** Never ending.

**lever** A piece that is used to operate a machine.

**material** Matter from which something is made.

**momentum** The force something has when it's moving.

**obstacle** Something that makes it difficult, or hard, to complete an action.

**smelt** To use heat to separate metals.

**spawn** In a video game, to appear or cause something to appear.

**transportation** A way of traveling from one place to another.

**venomous** Producing poison that can be used to harm other creatures.

# FOR MORE INFORMATION

## BOOKS

Miller, Megan. *Hacks for Minecrafters: Redstone*. New York, NY: Sky Pony Press, 2019.
Mojang AB. *Minecraft: Guide to Redstone*. London, UK: Dean, 2021.
Mojang AB. *Minecraft: Let's Build! Theme Park Adventure*. London, UK: Dean, 2019.

## WEBSITES

**Minecarts and Railway Systems**
*www.minecraft101.net/redstone/minecarts-and-railroads.html*
Learn more about minecarts and rails at this website.

**Tutorials/Minecarts**
*minecraft.fandom.com/wiki/Tutorials/Minecarts*
This page on the *Minecraft* wiki has a wealth of information on building railway systems.

**Types of Trains**
*www.timeforkids.com/k1/types-trains/*
Time for Kids describes types of real-world trains and railroads.

# INDEX


A
activator rails, 16

B
badlands, 8

C
creative mode, 18

D
detector rails, 16
dirt, 10

G
gold, 14
gravel, 10
gravity, 10

I
iron, 6, 7, 16

L
lava, 10, 11
lever, 17

M
minecarts, 4, 7, 8, 12, 13, 14, 15, 16, 18, 20
mineshaft, 8

O
ore, 6, 10, 14

P
powered rails, 14, 15

R
rails, 4, 6, 7, 8, 10, 12, 14, 15, 16, 17, 18, 20
redstone, 14, 16

S
sand, 10, 11
stone, 10, 11, 16, 17

W
water, 10, 11